IT'S
ABOUT TIME

PREVIOUS POETRY BY BARRY WALLENSTEIN

Tony's Blues, Éditions Pourquoi viens-tu si tard? 2020
Time on the Move, Xanadu Press, 2020
At the Surprise Hotel and Other Poems, Ridgeway Press, 2016
Drastic Dislocations: New and Selected Poems, NYQ Books, Feb. 2012
Tony's World, Birchbrook Press, 2010
A Measure of Conduct, Ridgeway Press, 1999
The Short Life of the Five-Minute Dancer, Ridgeway Press, 1993
Love and Crush, volume of poetry. N.Y. Persea Books, 1991
Roller Coaster Kid, T.Y. Crowell, 1982
Beast Is A Wolf With Brown Fire, Brockport, N.Y.: BOA Editions, 1977
Visions and Revisions: An Approach to Poetry, N.Y.: T.Y. Crowell, 1971
Visions and Revisions: The Poet's Process, [edited with Bob Burr]
    Broadview Press, 2002
Years of Protest: A Collection of American Writings of the 1930's,
    [edited with Jack Salzman] Pegasus, 1967
For Enid with Love: A Festschrift, edited; NYQ Books, 2010

RECORDINGS

Lisbon Sunrise [Sintoma Records, 2021]
Lisbon Sunset [Sintoma Records, 2018]
What Was, Was [Audioscope. 2015 LC 12366. Suisa]
Lucky These Days [Cadence Jazz Records CJR 1242; 2013]
I Carry Your Heart [BW's lyrics sung by Alexis Cole, Motema 2012]
Euphoria Ripens [Cadence Jazz Records CJR 1210. 2008]
Pandemonium [Cadence Jazz Records CJR 1194. 2005]
Tony's Blues [Cadence Jazz Records CJR 1124] 2001
In Case You Missed It, SkyBlue Records, CD # 106, 1995.
Taking Off, AK-BA Records, #1040, 1982. [Reissued on Bleu
    Regard records in France, 1995 as a CD]
Beast Is, AK-BA Records, #10200, poetry with music, 1978.

It's About Time

Barry Wallenstein

NY Books™

The New York Quarterly Foundation, Inc.
Beacon, New York

NYQ Books™ is an imprint of The New York Quarterly Foundation, Inc.

The New York Quarterly Foundation, Inc.
P. O. Box 470
Beacon, NY 12508

www.nyq.org

First Edition

Set in New Baskerville

Layout and Design by Raymond P. Hammond

Cover Design and Illustration by Carol McDonald

Author Photo © Roger Thomas

Library of Congress Control Number: 2021946293

ISBN: 978-1-63045-082-3

It's About Time

Acknowledgments

Grateful acknowledgment to the editors of the following journals and anthologies in which many of these poems originally appeared: *Manhattan Review; BigCityLit; Unlikely Stories; Live Mag; Poets Reading the News; Fell Swoop magazine #160; Home Planet News; Krytyka Literack* No. 3-4; *Like Light: 25 Years of Poetry & Prose by Bright Hill Poets & Writers; Siècle 21, Litterature & Societe; www.Eco-Poetry.org; Recours au Poème; Brilliant Corners; Albert Ayler: Testimonials on a Holy Ghost; Nueva York Poetry Review; Brownstone Poets; Acoustic Levitation.*

Special thanks to Barbara Rosenthal for publishing the chapbook *Time on the Move* (Xanadu Press 02.13.20) that contains nine poems that appear here.

Gratitude to Jean-Jacques Boin and the residency at Saorge, France for 15 seasons of peace and freedom to write.

Thanks to peer poets, Stephanie Rauschenbusch, Iris Lee, Helen Tzagoloff, Richard Schiffman, Jan Castro, Rosalie Calabrese, Alan Friedman, Michael Howley, Robert Burr, Joanna Chen whose monthly comments have helped many of these poems. Thanks as well to Jeffrey Cyphers Wright and Richard Levine for their excellent feedback.

Lorna Harbus Wallenstein, my first and always reader.

for Lorna, Daniel, Jessica, and baby Maya

CONTENTS

Eventually

Newborn ... 15
Time ... 16
Inventory ... 17
Yesterday, Today & Tomorrow ... 18
Autumn Leaf ... 19
Fast Fall ... 20
Diminishment ... 21
For Bob ... 22
Eventually ... 23
When Memory's a Treasure ... 24
Still Here ... 25
Friends on the Go ... 26
Tomorrow ... 27
Happy Birthday ... 28

Desire

Topsy-Turvy ... 31
Desire ... 32
Gender Play ... 33
Twins ... 34
Thus Far ... 35
An Idiot Chain ... 36
August Remembered ... 37
Love Point Blank ... 38
Swamp Girl ... 39
The Imp Speaks ... 40
Elf ... 41

Wind Advisory

Wind Advisory 45
Unfinished Dialogue 46
Stomach Ache 48
Anguish 49
Vengeance 50
Nightmare Fantasy 1 51
Nightmare Fantasy 2 52
Luminous Danger 53
Self-Help 54

Viewpoints

Simplicity 57
Wanderer 58
High Flier 59
Viewpoints 60
Instructions 61
On Shifting Sand 62
A Pinchpenny 63
Paradise Lane 64
The Walker 65
The Washer of Dishes 66
The Writer 68
Delights 69

Choice Morsels

The Wasp and Its Target 73
The Nightcrawler 74
Chance Performance 75
Mayflies 76
The Swift Leaves the Tree 77

Lifeboat

A Novel and Capricious Creature 81
Quarantined 82
Quarantined 2 /Longing 83
COVID Goes a Weeding 84
Lifeboat 85
Plague 86
The Backward Glance 87
Anxious Mother, Age 105 88

Headlines

A Broadside 91
Paradoxes 92
Sniper 93
Solarize the County 94
A Good Piss to Prevent a Spat 95
The Border 96
American Dream 97
Headlines 98

Old Man's Chatter

Files 101
Night Thoughts 102
Departure 103
Old Man's Chatter 104
Dawdling Past Curfew 105
Skin Deep 107
Elegy 108
Nick Johnson—a Remembrance 109
Unheard Words 110
Five Chairs in the Twilight Zone 111

The Rabbit Explains *112*
It's in the Bag *113*

Listen to the Music

Listen to the Music *117*
Lucky These Days *118*
Listening to Hal Galper at Club Bonafide *119*
For John Hicks *120*
Albert Ayler at the End of the Day *121*
"Bomb Cyclone" *122*
Little Ditty *123*
Improvisation *124*

Eventually

Newborn

She arrived late
but not later than ever,
not too late at all,
in fact, just in time.

Week one: I lift her
light as a thimble
but already a bundle.
I clasp her and rock her
in the hammock of my arms.

Maya is her name,
a bright star in the Pleiades,
a gem in Orion's Belt,
a golden gift as are my years.

Now and then she stretches, yawns
and blinks the lucent lids
that cover her blue/browns,
scarcely seeing after all that time
in the dark, out of town.

On granddad's first walk,
the soothing motion of the stroller
smooths the bumpety-bumps,
and puts her to sleep.
For the moment, she's oblivious
to urban disturbance and my world view.

Home again, mother and child preside,
as they do in drama and fiction.
History unfolds with every feeding,
every diaper change.

Time

Under every field of snow
lies a rising field of clover.

Remember we never wasted a moment—
not a jot lost in the rush—
your back room, an hourglass on its side.

"Yesterday I was five"
the six-year-old insists,
and at twenty the young man knows
that "yesterday I was five"
was true that day
and will always be.

The abandoned train rails rust
in the changing seasons' claw.
Still, do not play dead
on those antique tracks
as they bend around the hills,
flattening capsules of time;
watch for speeding trains
along the parallel bars.

Inventory

I have:
5 minutes left before the alarm
2 minutes left on the snooze button
a few pounds to lose
over the next short while
before the trip to bliss.

I've rubbed these two nickels together
and have a pile of dimes
higher than a house of cards.
I've a potted plant rich in loam
and plans in place
beyond the cancelled dates.

The cornucopia is no longer
overflowing. So...
those thin hands
know their way
around the clock's face.

Yesterday, Today & Tomorrow

Yesterday he was buoyant,
and he didn't need the waves
to float him above all care;
he stayed cheerful
all of that day,

and when he collided with an object,
it was painless; nothing ever broke.
The arms and hands he ran into
were embracing
and held him deep into evening.

Then morning arrived
but not on an aerial steed
flying joyously into the new day—
unease had come along
for the ride.

He slipped slowly into his personal nest,
a clock-watcher obsessed,
who laments the day for its dearth of hours.

Then, here it is again, time to go to bed again
and envision another tomorrow,
as if it were promised.

Autumn Leaf

From my image on the pond,
I know my blush is deep,
my edges curl,
and my stem, though attached,
is drying. I'll soon be on your surface.

Tonight's predicted rainstorm
may sail me to your topmost edge.
Once that happens—
the inescapable small tumble—
we'll be a spectacle of color.

But I'll hang here a little longer.
It may not rain after all,
so, there's extra time
while you wait for me.

Come spring
I could be lingering still,
the last leaf upon the tree.

Fast Fall

One day in summer
an alien from Mars or somewhere
landed and spoke to me
from his busy mouth:
"Your hours, like rats
will keep coming
and pile high as Everest,
before that long drop down,
too fast for you to frame
or see your minutes;
their delights fall with you."

Without a second to think or parry,
I reposted—remove your clock
and your foul mouth too -
back to where you came from;
I've enough hours in this world
but not a minute to waste
on your downward vision.

Diminishment

I need no gymnasium
no 12 steps in anyone's system

I'm a person of modest disposition
12 words a half-minute suit me
a few bites
a few drams
the last 3 inhalations
each time
is enough—

[that's how slight this time is,
and the story ends on twelve.]

For Bob

"Too late
to redo
or to do without"
my friend said in one of his sour moods,
disgruntled by choice,
while improving his skills on the mandolin.

"Not too late," I responded
in the middle of renovation:
placing this into that,
following the guide:
to do with
rather than without.

Not too late.
He rose from his recliner;
"to do without doing
may be the best trick for balance."

Eventually

the friendship will clarify or die,
the wound heal or fester,
the loose tooth tighten or fall out,
the falsehood reveal itself
and the fabricator be put in chains.

Eventually, the traffic will untie
and the bumpers locked together
will separate, and the cars will hum
along the freeway,
free in their release
all the way to Tuscaloosa.

Eventually, the seas will rise higher,
the stars come closer,
and a new species,
as full of chance as our own,
will rise up to build and knock down things
for a very long minute.

Eventually,
we'll ship out dressed like quality
to have a magic time in the coming months,
and our world, impressed by the wake of our passage,
will whisper within itself,
"maybe tonight."

When Memory's a Treasure

Nothing can be forgotten
that's never happened

so, kick the can, and I did
and now I remember it

tomorrow my memory will fasten
on an action taken

I'll build a table and place a plant
in the center, a Boston Ivy

that intakes CO_2
and sends out oxygen

but this lucky ivy has no memory;
its being is free of history

its fertile flowering stems
and the cells inside and out

mock my memory—
of what and why.

Still Here

I stumble upon each o'clock
crack my head upon a rock.

A monster reaches out of the bog,
hairy hands and flared nostrils;
its reach chills,
so, I blink back the danger
and look into my own amazing hands.

This pain, the tightening rings
of spinal awareness—signals naptime
at the chimes of afternoon.
Dreams come tumbling
into my daytime bedtime rest.

Children in the house around the clock,
lucky enough to repel the blow
or staunch the blood should it flow—
they're gone to where they go.

Friends on the Go

My friends and I walk nightly
into and out of the miasma,
tangled up in our own foolishness.
The little fish dart between our legs,
and we love them
for their silver slides.
In the day, we listen to new jazz
and Gregorian chants as we go.

Friends are gold coins
dropped into each of our pockets,
deep pockets with sensitive linings.
Each buys a round for the others
and when my turn comes around,
I'll toast to the times ahead.

Tomorrow

When that lovely word comes true,
the shadow that fooled no one lifts,
and we celebrate:
the gold comes teeming—
the morning stretch,
the fresh mouth after the brush,
for many—the first coffee or tea.
And then adventure begins
and proves the idea of tomorrow
grander even than luck or love
or holidays with no end of money.

Without tomorrow—as idea or fact:
no hook to hang anything,
no pot to piss in,
no pot no gin,
no kiss from mother, father, wife, or kids,
the old friend who drops by,
the new friend to embrace
and discover her story;
no taste on the tongue
no bitter aftertaste to spit
no failed memory—but to become one.

Banish the thought that blocks the rhythm;
advancing age supports the pretense of wisdom.

Happy Birthday

Maya—9 months
(that funny word) old.
You've been outside now
longer, a bit, you beauty,
then you were inside—
your observations
considerations ruminations
while in the dark and in the light
remain unavailable to us;
we'll someday know your preferences,

but your bright smile
on the edge of a chuckle,
signals joy.
The occasional howls
suggest not the opposite
but something else—
fathoms below and above the stars.
Those cries or sighs
buoy us up as we
pick you up to hold,
nestle and fool around.

Suddenly—you're crawling—
wretched is the world
that missed the moment.
And a day ago—speech!
Ba ba ba, and did I hear Hi
in response to my Hi?
Possibly yes, but in time
you'll say much more—
including rude words
with accompanying gestures.
For now, there's ba ba ba ba
and clapping
at 9 months and counting.

Desire

Topsy-Turvy

Wandering lonely atop a cloud
I fell into a turvy.
A cart pulled by three dappled horses—
      one named Topsy
      one called Heat
      and the last one Miss Cool—
passed me by, and the iron wheels
churned up a mist of dust.

So here I am,
in the mid-stride of my age
all upside down in love.
One day her smile is like a quilt
cozy and warm to slip under;
the next day her grin askew
with lust and discontent
sends me into the curve of a spin.

What to do when spell-bound,
with all those years behind me
and a few up ahead?
I call her, and my heart catches
with each brief ring of sound.
Her voice trills in the receiver,
and I'm lost once more to be found.

Desire

I sleep with a yellow lady
rolled up into a pill
each milligram a promise
of what to touch on waking,
each promise a lie
under disproving light.

She left me alone for a time,
but I wasn't lost, just sick.
The doctor nearly cut my scripts.
A leaden time went by
before her return. So startling it was
I had to rub myself to recall
she'd been gone.

Life now at home is a banquet
of massage: the neck, the back
even the backs of our thighs
revel under her touch.
The doctor knows this
and winks at me and my partner,
the yellow lady on the table,
and I don't understand a thing.

Gender Play

Asexual? Bisexual? Gay?
Trans? On occasion?
Hardly, but a woman when wished for—
keeps him/herself generally clean
and slips into something sleek and comfortable
for an occasion.

After descending from her mountain,
she'll hold him in her arms and,
breathing close to his ear,
release a floral tongue,
a lovely thing that teases lightly
then grows willowy branches
for children to climb.
They don't play there long;
they drop to the ground where the grownups tilt
and dash off to who knows where,
while the mountain climber and her beau
advance towards a house
where a room full of men and women
and a lizard too,
wait for their arrival—
a stunning twilight in mid-afternoon.

Twins

He was born a twin
but solitary—brotherless, sisterless,
an odd number, a one.

Soon he twinned
with every breathing being:
the mother, the father,
a sleepy neighbor stopping by,
the family cat,
and as soon as they exchanged glances,
they gained his look,
his features, his budding frame,
his attitude.

At four, when they sat him down for dinner,
cleaned up and perky,
all his twins imagined aging—
but with their ages somehow on hold.
One took on his lack of doubt,
another—his bounding health,
and the last, the cat,
his bristling, burgeoning capacity
to lick and to love.

Thus Far

So far, we've not been together
long enough
for the distant bell's ringing
to thin in the wind
or become tangled filament
in memory's wild hair.

It takes a year or more
for the sheep to fatten,
meat to be sliced,
placed on the plate, eaten,
and each gravied morsel savored.

As our meal baked,
we talked, basted and added spices.
The wait was less heavy
than lint on a blind man's coat.
The minuscule wrinkles and portents
slept in the shadows.

Neither of us have thighs
that are shudder-proof
or wise to the number of days
allowed in the arc of
what we've built
in this intemperate season.

Thus far, our lamps' red wicks
burn on two flames;
slowly they go down
leaving the scent of paraffin,
while the sparks flicker
then glow.

An Idiot Chain

He's besotted by bliss: fresh water
and a leak-proof roof, no debt.
The air around him—
the odors, even the funk
coming off his body—
send him to heaven.
His pluses balance well
against the minuses he pretends
are missing or locked in sleep;

but he despises the one misery:
his right arm chained to the wall,
as if he'd run away
or abuse himself were he not so shackled.
His overseers are professional
and pretend to be kind—
from time to time.
He rails against his chain—calls it an idiot—
ringed to the mottled wall.

Then, weary of such a state,
he yanks free from his idiocy;
the chain rattles, falls and retracts.
He bolts from the room;
sniffing the air,
he begins his slow but avid search,
first close to home then out of town,
for candidates to share his bliss.

August Remembered

We rode a bicycle built for two
and tried to stay under the leaves
and peddle in the shade
but there was only half shade.

At the end of the ride,
we disembarked and then stripped.
This was the heat we'd dreamt of
all through winter and the chilly spring.

After dinner, dressed again,
we entertained our evening,
just ourselves, a friendly audience,
mutually enamored at having lasted this long.

Then, we slid between the lily whites
and fed our night on the day's delights.

Love Point Blank

She loves me between the eyes
I feel it, but her world calls her
dizzy.

I wish she'd pull the trigger
and stop the tease that makes me
dippy.

I could love her right back
and with wit, desire and
artistry

right between the gazangas;
live in that mood
so happily.

Pull that trigger oh my dear
wipe away the drift towards
iffy;

let's settle down—have a family—
a dinette in place; a silver
privy.

A conversation, lascivious play,
then, the next day, poetically,
a little fishy.

Your itchy finger's pressed down;
the bullet's on its way—
it's not too risky.

Swamp Girl

What was a brown and green grove,
is now a spectacle of cockeyed ferns.
Dank patches smudge the lawn's edge;
moss thickens up to the snake holes.

Growing one on the other,
red maples and birches couple up.
Rootlegs intertwine and lightly test
her sponge-like membrane.

Pink fluted mushrooms rise
along the way; puckered lips
wet the crevices of rotting stumps,
but she recalls only the finest weather.

Her skirt becomes muddy & slimy;
spiders stealthily weave about her shoulders.
She's languid but alert
in the new-found vegetable kingdom.

The Imp Speaks

I may be too pooped to prove the point,
as we say in the lands of frolic,
but I'm still perky
and can do the do
when my turn comes around,

and also climb the banyan tree
limb by limb to where the snake and tiger
wrap themselves in the myth of the manger;
and should you call up "when you reach the top,
toss me a kiss with your fingers."

I'll do just that—with the spark I've left,
though more tired by then than I can ever remember.

Elf

My handy randy household elf
has left me
lonely
with the front door ajar
and his shadow dancing
down the lane.

So, I slipped the bolt,
set the alarm, and
in the newfound sullen solitude
alphabetize my collections,
arrange and rearrange
all the objects within reach.

If I were a jar on the shelf,
empty, translucent
I'd ask for water and a flower
and then placement in the center
of the harvest table,
but he's not here.

I miss his presence—handy randy
helper around the house
full of quips and gentle tricks
dressed in silk or tweeds,
an elfin smile that could unlock
or lock again any door or troubled mind.

Wind Advisory

Wind Advisory

He was cautioned,
while raking the leaves
to mistrust the wind,
east wind west wind;
any breeze across the yard
could upset his piles
and set him behind once again.
Even one leaf blown from the heap
would jinx the arrangement
and jitter his nerves.

And then she warned further:
there could be turbulence,
swirling currents of fury.
So, he feared the house,
its ivories, wall hangings,
and all that he loved
would be blown away
and smashed to debris,
with no one left in the neighborhood
to restore all that was.

This Casandra with her auguries,
issued in syrupy tones,
was herself an arbiter of winds,
a windbag of worries;
they were a strange pair
living in so many zones.
Even in fair weather
she sensed the storm coming.

Unfinished Dialogue

I've come all this way across town
through the tunnel, over the bridge,
down the narrow alley to your door,
for the purpose of murder.
You tonight and then I'll do myself
later on; I've had enough of everything
and more than enough of you.

All this and from an old friend,
a brother I'd call him sometimes.
For years, I put up with his bluster;
he'd look past my vacuity,
and we'd love each other that way.
Now, seeing the terror in his eyes,
my terrified voice squeaks "Why?"

Because you are you and not me
sharp slivers of iron cut in my brain,
which was tolerable for a long time,
but now the rust is driving me mad,
and hatred rides high on its galloping
stallion. I'm in the saddle with a whip,
a rifle and hand gun, and now is our time.

OK, wait I say; just listen for a minute -
I was in the middle of writing you
a letter of memories: do you remember
our boat trips, acid trips, the guilt trips
we never took yet joked about?
Do me one last kindness:
you suicide first and I'll catch up later.

Continued >

Very funny, but I've heard that one before
in a movie we watched together
in an open-air theater,
but that was a long time ago
and I've lost my good humor.
The old jokes are sour and I'm about to
pull the trigger.

NO, wait a half-minute
while I sweat and shake for you;
I see your cause is true,
your anger and determination, marvelous,
but at the end of this episode,
you'll be off the page,
while I continue to scribble and erase.

Stomach Ache

I know, despite their silence,
there's activity.
This group of magic scoundrels,
punctilious scalawags, putzerinos,
is inflicting ague and pinches.
They're pleasuring themselves
inside my system, just below the waist.

My once sovereign space
is now a frame of opportunity
for this fraternity of roamers
with spiked heels and spurred boots
who leave their detritus and indentations
all over my innards' red and pink walls.

Even were this intrusive population slow,
somewhat still, or neutral,
I'd resent the trespass
as I resent my bellyaching.

Anguish

Born on the inside of a pin
he soon developed a hatred of pricks
and narrow places; his stormy moods thundered,
and he was lost in the passages.

Padded cells failed to cushion his fury.
His family tried, the state tried too,
and every time the wild horses returned
he rode them and leapt the fences.

There are days, the sanguine few,
when the tempest subsides;
periods of calm trap the steam,
and he sleeps deeply in those spaces:

holding stations, where nothing explodes,
and there is no frightened sorrow,
no bruised hands or trembling broken hearts
over the failed economies of his life.

Vengeance

Having been ripped off too often,
I've trained animals with extraordinary teeth
to bite and stay true to me
and to their natures.
These creatures—my team, my squadron—
exist in all sizes.

The ferret, for example,
is two feet long and fierce.
I place the big fella (no danger to myself)
on the axe handle hanging from the wall
near to where someone walked off
with my hand sledge.

Should the creep who stole my tool,
(he must have come creeping)
try to steal my axe: watch out!
My ferret will dart up his sleeve,
spit arm chunks and won't let go
till the thief backs out empty-handed

to the extreme.
Then he'll see through the glare
of this bloody spectacle,
a phalanx of beasts large and small
flexing their chops.

Nightmare Fantasy 1

I'm placed on this 30° slope,
looking down.
They've provided a pair of skis,
a costume and called me a hero
at the top of my curve;
I'm dizzy looking down
at the sheer, steep carpet of white.

This is a platform designed and
inclined for professionals
in bright colors,
not a fan of fine wool and scarves
who's a stranger to snow
and slippery hills.

So, why am I here
performing in a farce
imposed upon me
in front of a jury of three?
One is a professor of ornithology
a bird-brain himself
in league with the other two,
a sports photographer
and an undertaker.
They're ready for what will happen.

It's been an hour, and now
finally, I see them moving
in my direction; cameras are rolling,
the crowd is restive.
Suddenly, I'm flying downhill.
The trees, so stationary a second ago,
gather speed as I ski
lighter and lighter as if to safety—
without a silk net to catch me
or break the fall.

Nightmare Fantasy 2

My son at four
saw the slimy green hand
catch at my left leg and cause me to stumble
into a hole in the ground.
I smiled, looking up from five-feet deep,
a foot and a half of water at the bottom,
where beneath the already churning muck
I was being held. I smiled,
not wanting to see terror in his face
magnified by my own.

So, I calmly raised my voice for help—
run I yelled—now—
and for a minute or so he froze,
not wanting to leave the solid
but slipping me.

He ran as I kicked and splashed
aiming my kicks at the unseen
hands or claws: suddenly
I felt the ooze open,
and grabbed a scaly arm
(which detached so easily I fell back)
and hurled it out of the pit.
Another appeared, and I wrenched it lose
and flung it out as well.

Each arm I tossed rooted in the ground,
and in the midst of my winning struggle
and my boy's valiant run,
trees like canopies
sprung from the earth,
providing shade on this field,
where, tomorrow,
father and son may meet.

Luminous Danger

The Wolf Moon, full of itself,
looms over this January field,
snow-covered and sparkling.
The creatures are silent
careful not to shatter the spell.

Some lie snugly asleep
in their hibernated dens,
caves and cavities; others
test the silence
in their stealth.
Their paws leave prints
humans will not follow.

There's no one visible,
but the packs lurk around
imagining ways to intrude.

Here's a lonesome cabin
deep in the valley.
The shades are drawn
against the moonlight.
Outside the Wolf Moon
illuminates all paths
of possible flight.

Self-Help

Beneath his scarf
and smarting disposition
he tries to stop snuffling.

Excessive lamentation,
he knows, would leave him
salty and. spent.

Hurry out of the house
into the garden
where soft stems
extend then harden.

He feels a wet frond,
an overgrown root;
he smells dank darkness,
props up the wilted fern with his thumb.

He stifles another tear
then smooths the shirt
that protects the skin
that covers his heart.

No one sees him walk in
to brew a tea,
pick up a novel,
slip into neutral.

Viewpoints

Simplicity

Bread and cheese
salt on something
quiet conversation
gin over ice
beads on a yellow string
ganga or call it muta or muggles;

an apple, honey in a dish
a free afternoon in good weather.
A memory that persists
until now; the train
that stops at every station
is slow but on time.

Keep it simple: a straight line
or, if needed, a circle;
the urge toward perfection
belongs to the body too and
issues from the same place
as sweat.

Wanderer

Facing two paths, one named Maybe,
the other one called For Sure,
he selects the best bet and steps forth.

Maybe leads somewhere, not everywhere,
but it's on a tilt and he's the marble
moving on a table in the aftershocks of a quake.
His stomach unsettles; yet his reddened eyes
see well-enough to find a match
to light the smoke waiting to be sparked.

For Sure leads every place he steps;
and he strides with fresh assurance
up the path to grab a ring
and down the road to hand it over.
He has chances in his pockets,
enough to spend or give away.

High Flier

From out the bay window,
they could see me rise
then ride off on a thermal
higher than ever.

From this height
I cannot read their faces.
Are they amazed yet fearful
that I might drift the way of high-flying birds
hawks or falcons?

After performing the tail whip,
delighted in mid-air, I descend
to attend to my hunger.
The soft landing settles my system
ahead of the meal.

Now I walk in the door
and see the arrangement:
three deadpan faces,
no bright hugs or celebration.
It's as if I'd never taken flight.

Viewpoints

From one angle
the giant is forcing its weight
onto the shoulders of the toad,
a smaller giant to the mites below;
it's been hours of such imposition.

From another point of view,
the toad need not weep;
he's alive and feels the weight.
His sticky tongue still flicks out
turning flies into juice,

sustenance that allows the toad
(though fools call him frog)
to jump away;
his sweat makes him slippery
and hard for the giant to hold.

Will the giant lament
as he lumbers out of the muck,
his footprints puddling the mud?
He never saw the toad; caught up in his being,
ignorance protects him from shame.

Who is Giant?
Grandpa? no, he's been gone
for ages. Father, the nurturing colossus?
Why not?
He is pressure on all he loves.

Instructions

Bereft of company,
check the mirror, pucker up,
and blush for shame
before I come in to comment.

Find a friend
and climb the ladder.
Look around and then come down.
Scale the mountain without ropes.
Return to the earth
and don't say a word.

Listen to me—a better angel—
your best bet in times of fury,
come winter and the first snow,
make a snowball,
tighten it icy hard
and let it melt in your hands.

Hold on to your pricelessness.
Wake to your meager weight,
squeeze what it is into a thimble,
fondle your likeness to the worm.

Alight on the nearest tree;
see the next person
seated on the branch.
Fly off together
over the lake's rim.
Land and climb back to the branch
alone, and smile like a baby.

On Shifting Sand

He covers his nature
with a coat of confidence,
a dash of arrogance,
a charm that dulls the audience,
hand-picked and pliant.

He stumbles into an afterlife
where everything—tip to toe
repeats itself, as before;
and stumble he will
back to himself

where he wishes the winter light
he basks in
not suffer a disruption of service,
for it's the service he counts on
in his paradise:

the seas awash with provender—
variety on his plate.
A monkey, or a devil,
appears with a napkin;
a toad hops up with a dram of gin.

This man walks on fluid sands
and embraces the weather,
all weather as it happens
except for the cyclone
that could spin him off the earth

and away from his friends,
pockets of quiet and
the planet's havoc;
he'd rather not leave again
and maybe never return.

A Pinchpenny

Slim-cat the Skinflint
deprives himself sweets,
walks a mile to save a fare,
tries to squeeze dimes out of pennies,
and he dreams up his own movies,
pops his own corn.

His lovers call him thrifty,
his friends call him frugal;
those who see him tight with his wad
never ask to borrow, pass him by
and giggle over his zipped-up pockets,
his squinty eyes and shady look.

He knows how to flake the flint
'till thin as skin, but, here comes a figure
with charisma and charm enough to loosen his fist,
and pry the dollars from his hand.
He's flinty still, but now he buys roses
for this friend—oodles of roses.

Paradise Lane

To the left of the stump
where five branches had bloomed,
until blight brought them down,
is a walkway called Paradise Lane.

This path defies definition
as it weaves and narrows forever.
People walk there arm in arm, well-armed
well-dressed, an intermittent diamond among them.

With cautious chit chat and the clearing of throats,
handsome bodies glide amidst abundant nature;
the lane itself slips around its name
as easily as a child plays hide and seek.

The Walker

He vowed to the crowd
to put some mileage on his legs,
and the concomitant parts
with all the weight they carry.

He walked from bed to table,
changed from house slippers
to high tops—well-cushioned
and leading him on.

He stepped out into the city
with long-strides and a steady pace—
from south to north—west to east—
saw storefronts, lamp lights and dark windows.

There was not a bench he spied
that he didn't regard
and then disregard
as he walked further on.

A ball game exploded in the park;
excited fans,
focused on the score,
missed him walking by.

Undaunted, he tracked the miles—
a mission to stick to—
until the app fails
or the pedometer ages out.

The Washer of Dishes

He doesn't need much,
not a new dwelling,
not a new occupation,
but he does need a kitchen sink
over which he can
open the spigot, wet the sponge
squeeze on soap, flex the hands,
urge the shoulders into it,
fully engage all the musculature
of the upper body.

He's fast, but it's been years
since he's timed himself
scrubbing through a tub of dishes,
glasses, pots & pans,
riveted—a quixotic focus.
He used to count off seconds
as he scrubbed one glass
after another; now he loses count
in the act of drying.

To avoid the dangers
of splintered crockery, blood on a knife,
he employs the right grip—
a balance between tight
and super-careful,
for all the soapy surfaces
challenge his flesh.

Continued >

After the music stops
and the kitchen's clean
and everything's put away,
he crowns himself
Prince of the Dishes.

When young,
he was kept out of the kitchen—
no man's land.
Now he's master of that universe,
but he's developing a reputation.

The Writer

The fountain pen had a few flaws
and leaked words onto the page
and blurred the line
that ran into danger—

too high a speed
for such a slick road—
gravel on the shoulders.
So, the vehicle—new & clean
spun over—twice—hit a tree,
landed upside down—totaled.
The driver survived.

The writer loves his pen
despite the leakage.
He also likes cleaning up
the writing implement,
the table, his shirt and pants;
but what he likes best
is dipping the gold nib
into the bottle of blue ink
and making the bladder fill up—
a reservoir for lines to come.

Delights

Charles the Bold banished enchantments
but embraced these few delights:

Inhaling   fresh air
or a passing aroma
the scent of sweat after a tumble
the aftermath of engagement

Listening   to incarnations
of music made centuries ago
hummed by someone drunk on melody
and the bridges in-between

Observing   the sight of a 3-legged dog's leap
towards a boy—his arms embrace;
he strokes and scratches
but nowhere near the disappeared limb

Savoring   certain cheeses
Wenselydale Blue, Gjetost from Norway,
firm of texture and brown by design;
stinky Limburger

Driving   into the outer boroughs
top down as in the olden days—
the radio lost in the wind
until the car slows and the music ascends

Obeying   elders (when they can be found);
their wisdom, natty attire, witty palaver
should be packaged, and passed down
to the children of the new world

Choice Morsels

The Wasp and Its Target

After I left the screen-door open,
a wasp paid me a visit,
and, at first, I thought he'd come alone,
but as time passed,
I saw the sky darken
and heard the hum.

Clearly, he'd invited friends,
and they landed—eyed me
as if I were nectar
or some flower they'd heard about
up in the rafters where they nest and breed.
Then I go down to the village and try to be sweet,
but too wary of moving objects
and the daily news to be truly delicious.

The Nightcrawler

I am one of the night-crawlers
seeking, while slithering along,
the many flavors of the earth.

Some see me a greedy sucker,
and when walkers look down,
they hesitate; some step around

my moving form;
others don't halt their careless stride
and could make a mess of what's inside.

The steppers see us as clones,
multiples twining our way over
and into the earth.

A foolish observation—
I'm distinguishable, visible
to those humble enough to bow

down and touch the soil
with cheek and nose eye to eye
with my slow slink.

Pushed to the wall
I'll find the way to the tastes
that compose my time:

bitter, sweet; sour & salty;
astringent, too, tastes just right
for this hermaphrodite.

On a cloudy afternoon when in the woods
step carefully,
permit envy to enter your minds.

Chance Performance

A white pillar of sand stands
close by the New Infirmary;
mica flecks glint and shimmer.

The sand fly, despite her broken wing
and all that distance flown,
knows she's the luckiest moving object
in the territory.

Mayflies

I dread the black flies of spring
and their inevitable bites.
They offer no amulet for protection,
no plan for what's to come.

A flatcar points downhill
loaded with freight
strapped down for the ride.
Only a miracle will save the conveyance.

The trudge uphill after the ride
will be arduous with many stops
that attract buzzing swarms.
I dread the metaphor.

The Swift Leaves the Tree

Near the close of a dream
I heard the words "the trees give birds,"
and I woke with a wish
to find one bird prescient enough
to absolve the tree
that had sheltered it from life
to chick to fledgling to flight.

No such bird appeared,
and the tree remains unforgiven,
but in full leaf,
as grand as a house
with many rooms
emptied of the children
who have flown the clichéd nest.

One bird, the swift,
hardly out of the shell,
leaves the tree;
once up in the air
it mates on the wing
and stays aloft.

Lifeboat

A Novel and Capricious Creature

Covid the Cobra
slithers by the barn—
spits its invisible venom
in no one's direction,
but the drafty air wafts it
to mingle
with the lilac's aroma.

The ring-necked cobra
rears back and opens its hood
when disturbed;
when undisturbed,
like all things menacing,
it waits and glistens
with potential.

Though other snakes
possess more potent virulence,
Mister or Miss Cobra
can send out enough neurotoxin
to finish off 20 people in a flash
or one elephant.

The iconic Cobra,
elegant in posture and nature,
demands respect. At ease
it likes its time underground,
but disregard drives it
and sends killer bits of matter
into the open where all are at risk.

Quarantined

I've choked my imagination,
blocked all the passages into
and away from
this awareness.

My mind now
spawns a wilderness
where birds and beasts
hunker down and listen

to the dulcet melodies
of last year's frolic,
last year's thoughts
and today's digressions.

Once the gates are opened,
I'll tip-toe outside,
and on a whim
choose a direction,

or imitate the phoebe's
darting flight.

Quarantined 2 / Longing

Confined
I long to look back
on a slice of buckled time.

Sequestered
and protected—yet
the comeuppance may creep in.

Skeletal forms, then vapors
advance in all directions,
invisible.

A dreadful stirring in the air:
particles liberated
from an excited center

and settling in our lives—
might as well be a tongue
on its way to intimate.

One day I shall recall this longing
and this blighted time.

COVID Goes a Weeding

First, I remove the Elders,
then the halt and the lame,
then those in tents or huts,
favelas, shanties,
slums.

I know my way around,
and when the pruning's done,
I'll vanish for a while,
smile in my corner,
and allow the players
back into their games.

But, then I'll return to do my duty:
to winnow the population—
separate the mighty
from the less-so.

There are still the young blades
who can't imagine my blades,
the brave teens,
toddlers in the pink;
my clipping shears go snip snap.

Lifeboat

Once in need of a lifeboat
to carry him from war
to the region of peace,
he shopped along the wharf.

Two young men,
glanced sideways with a smile,
directed him to the boatman's shack,
a derelict structure on stilts.

An inner tube with patches
sat beneath the salesman's porch;
a wooden sign with hand-drawn letters
announced the sale:

"Half-price—will float
just like a lifeboat."

Plague

The population is alive,
its enemies within
and without—threatening in.
There's a bug going 'round
taking names;
its preferences are unknown.

I can easily sleep deeply
twice a day
and wake lively enough
to endure the storm
that has us all battened down
and hiding.

I can still touch the objects
set upon the table
and move them carefully
even while the tables turn
on our species,
so privileged for so long.

I can rub the itch that's new
and, hopefully, be rid of it
before it spreads and baffles me further.
What joy to be free of it
personally and politically.
I'd celebrate deeply if quietly.

The Backward Glance

I tried to escape the fire
before it licked into the crevasses
of this city and quickly singed
the outer boroughs
and beyond to the wheat fields
where the farmers shield their faces.

First, I attempted to step around it,
then flew fast through it,
but once past the flame
I looked back as did Lot's wife,
and so, froze.

Now I try to forget the blaze
right here under our feet
shaping halos above our heads.
This consummation has cancelled
the shows, even the open-air pageants,
and soon every display of sobriety.

Anxious Mother, Age 105

In the midst of this raging contagion,
we're worried about our son. He's 80,
with health issues
a target for the microbes,
and he flouts the rules:
he refuses to self-quarantine,
he refuses to wear a mask
and he sneaks into boarded-up bars
to invite strangers in
for free booze and hugs.
Even at our age, we worry.

He was a rambunctious child,
a troubled teen
a wild intemperate youth
scattering his seed
here and there
and into the outer boroughs.

Well, he survived those years
and came out OK
able to feed himself
and finally, in the middle of his life,
a family.
We watched his every stage.

And we're watching still
from a distance, of course,
isolated centenarians. We Zoom in
to say we love you,
and remind him about life's fragility.
Aging's not what it used to be.

Headlines

A Broadside

The grass cries "the earth beneath tastes different."
The tree breathes "the air's sweet—a final magic."

The gentleman who tosses a ball to an imaginary friend
will contribute to the cause when he settles down,
creates a list, and finds his checkbook.

The streams gurgle "we're drying down and away."
The oceans surge "we're high tide and warning."

The couple in the yard climbs into their hammock;
their fingers entwine while they lament the issues
that cause such dissent and distress.

The whale belches "fish oil I remember; not this emollient."
The bear bellows "I've left my cave weeks ahead, and I'm lost."

The partygoers argue but then succumb
to sluggish lingering, while the commanders
are full of certainty and velocity.

Paradoxes

"Isn't tyranny a kind of oblivion?"
texted a friend from out of town.
I didn't know how to respond or calm down
and finish my meditation on Zeno's paradox.

Split the distance *ad infinitum* and never get there:
Achilles shamed by the tortoise in the race.
So again, no oblivion;
the hand never comes close enough to clap.
The revelers at the carnival are never gone.

Sniper

Now, at the end of his employment,
his fingernails keep him awake.
He envisions them growing faster,
faster than grass;
his phobic block
against clipping, he fears,
will endanger how he's remembered.

Already they've grown beyond
the short lives of his targets.
Soon his fingers will sport hooks
at their ends.

He'll take those nails with him,
he says, at the end of his day
when new grasses will have come up,
(the lush coverall under which
he'll lie)
while the nails still grow for a while.

His trigger finger's useless,
except to point or to scratch,
without a target to consider.

Solarize the County

Energy from the Sun and Wind today
will not dim the sunshine
or slow the wind tomorrow.
The force of the river,
caught by a wheel, will not be diminished.

A human chain circles the power plant,
as citizens visualize
how to turn the pipes into windmills
and refine the notion of refinery.

Solar panels shine in the fields,
converters off to the side;
electric boxes and meters
keep the tally.

Amidst our wild and serene rivers,
the acres of high hills and gullies,
seasons continue.
We play in our corner
with the time that's given.

A Good Piss to Prevent a Spat

The animal marks its territory well
with a piss—urine so strong and pungent,
unambiguous and calm—
that it creates a pasture for the spirit;

kindred spirits float above the markers.

The fences, walls, and boundaries
of human design, piss-less affairs,
are doomed to fall the way of nations
with wayward intentions;

flowers set along the borders shrivel.

No safety in the drawn lines
or the walled borders.
Delusional indications!

The Border

The guards, filed teeth,
eyes neither warm nor cold,
are armed and armored
against would-be travelers.

So, no one moves forward.
The crowds at the checkpoint
thicken and stamp.

But then, like a miracle,
faint music hovers over;
boundaries collapse—
stones become smooth sand,
and barbed wires rust away.

Where did it come from,
this tune with its swing tones melodic
that carries a strand of souls
across the border to meet and greet
the others?

It came from a town
called Fearless
where the people are various
and polylingual.
They circle and open all day long.

American Dream

The boy, now a man,
raised on chain-linked avenues
of lonely city # 3
or blasted city # 4—
worked himself bloody-handed
out of one flat into a larger one
curtains and flatware
and then to a suburban house
drapes and china
and then a larger one with a yard
and a boat up on blocks
and so on up the ladder
and each time now
his hands become a little cleaner.

Headlines
Autumn 2018

Torrents of Gunshot Shift Reality

In some districts, the light fractures
and dims; human shapes rise
to crawl toward a fearsome
and embraceable target.

Deadly Attack in Nairobi

A fist rises, then a banner,
while a loud voice dissembles.
Massed militias are motivated,
and they move forward, tight jaws.

Saudi War Pushes Yemenis to the Brink of Starvation

A Monday foresaw a Friday;
a Friday remembered a Monday.
The pattern promised respite,
a walk in the park, community.

Political Rage Grew in South Florida Loner

Populations are steamrolled,
bulldozed back to
the two left bewildered
standing in the ruined garden.

Bomb Suspect Found Identity in Resentment

The End of Days is a braggart myth.
Adorers of the moon,
the leader and his minions
bow to Disorder.

Old Man's Chatter

Files

Professor once, *emeritus* now,
he bends over his files—
old notes boxed in old oak—
pulls them out by their worn tabs
and tosses bunches into the fire
in a hurry, with august anger
and a self-mocking grin.

      "That's that for that,"
he chortles, clearing out obsolescence.
There's a long pause before some premonition
swings into focus.
      "One ending need not presage another"
is another sentence he likes to repeat.

So he sits straight-backed,
his fingers twiddling,
practicing his yo-yo
and conjuring time beyond limits
where, through the doors of the nearby workshop
he hears mice sing, men chirp,
and women romance the moon,
while mouthing aloud a randy tune.

Night Thoughts

Lately, in the night,
I'm the best sleeper in town.
Once I shut my eyes
I'm out for a solid stretch,
dead to the world
as the saying goes.

With this kind of sleep-ability,
I'll no doubt do death
as well as I do sleep,
so well
it will outlast lifetimes.

It's the only thing in the world
that goes on forever,
as the comedian once said
to a laughing, applauding audience.
Enough jokes: no more dreaming,
no more little snores,
restless leg jumps,
drool in the corners of slack lips.

For some poor souls, that final shut-eye
is the perfect hiding place,
better than sleep;
for others, it's a scam.

Departure

Dying is departure art.
Disallowed in the morgue,
it shows up, or is presented,
on the streets, in museums,
theaters, where we live.

And the audience devours it;
from curtain rise to curtain fall,
pleasures extenuate.
Resumption, the art of returning,
is a delusionary delight.

At the finale, someone yells
"put the body in the cart
and wheel it off and away
before it turns rotten,
an affront to the nose night and day."

So it goes, and go it does
until a pinch, an ache settles in,
and the waning begins,
though some say it began long ago
during that first act entrance.

Old Man's Chatter

In this shortest of seasons
I play my cameo role
and zip about
as if forever were a dance
I could still dance.

If I had my druthers,
I'd tag an hour on to each day
and on Sundays tag on two.
I'd be grateful beyond greed
to have the time to tell my tale.

The leap year is a good idea
and I count on it,
but a one-day bonus every 4 years
seems paltry, an insult to my desire,
which grows as the moon climbs.

Under this generous sky
I've light enough to read by,
but would rather polish the silver,
and set the clock, then move everything
to its rightful space.

Then I'll be tired but not too tired
to drink the potion required
to preserve my health for another day,
a day with plans
and a lot to do after breakfast.

Dawdling Past Curfew

Surely it was an error or a lucky punch
that let me slip through
and continue in this living room,
the best room on the planet,
when the others have left,
some few, years ago
some others, just lately.

They no longer know I'm here
in the room, or maybe,
possessed by magic,
some do know
and think my way,
feel into the corners
of this large room.

It cools a little
every time someone leaves.
All the coats, hats, scarves,
neatly hung in the closet,
are bored on their hangers,
devoid of utility.

So, I stick around
and envision my needs,
palpate my hunger,
photograph all I can,
find the music
that keeps me listening
and in touch with the players.

Continued >

Out this plate glass window
beauties pass by,
a phoebe, a falling feather,
a postal worker with parcels;
boys and girls who vibrate
on the verdant lawn.
The past tense makes no sense.

Skin Deep

When, seeing through the skin
to the bones visible in his hand
on a certain day
when all thought was tenuous,
threading out from the spool,
veering towards gloom,
he turned his eyes away
toward a stack of nudes
pictured on playing cards
in front of Mr. Luck
in a fine black suit
used to winning at cards, dice,
or any game of chance—
a man near in weight to himself.

The apparent similarity
of one person to another,
took his mind off skeletons
and back to the quotidian:
pay some bills, toss some others—
the floor to scrub
where the dog had made a mess,
or was it his error to keep a dog
at his age and at this address?

The hand rests palm down;
the skin,
a translucence of blue veins
slightly swollen,
a swim in the shallows,
a hush, inaudible heart thrum,
a gush of blood, a wash over bone.
He takes a quick look before bedtime
and a more studied look before sleep.

Elegy

for Nick Johnson

your face—once pale white
on the pillow as are your bones now
long exanimate—from the ride, the pang, the desire

ex-animate—the players
ex-animate—the stars
ex-animate—the tyrants

ex-animate—the city itself
ex-animate—firebombs and airwaves
ex-animate—the contestants
ex-animate—prayer

your face—colors vibrant and foreseen -
animates all flesh—
the famous, the dressed up, the natural fool,
in a whorl of recall

Nick Johnson—a Remembrance

His voice, infectious, inimitable
catches in my throat:
"Vodka martinis straight up
and a plate of unsalted fries."

"Time to leave," he would say,
drawing on a cigarette and
"Don't get me wrong" and
"The way I see it."

We'd swap radio bits from childhood:
late night Jean Shepard
(so important) and Mystery Theater,
(not important at all).

He left finger prints, toe prints,
medical bills, other bills and
the lines that came out of his mouth
and penned in ink on paper.

Now a mark on the calendar—
the first anniversary
of when his heart failed
to allow him another day.

His body conspired
against his self
for a too long lingering while,
and then the connections failed.

If the cycle were different,
he'd come back to us,
put on a clean shirt and tie
and his Trilby hat set at an angle.

Unheard Words

Poppa, I confess
I stole the boats
but I promise,
they will be returned.
A damaged burden on my mind
since you left.

With my small frame
and cherished smoke,
I travel past your marker,
place a stone on my way,
and the silence makes sense,
though I berate it.

Back in the hotel
far from home
far from whatever was said,
I bump my head
and imagine some injury,
a bloody bruise,
will wake you from the dead.

Five Chairs in the Twilight Zone

We players, all in our final chapter,
do not fail to fill
the five empty chairs
spaced around the living room,
first with ghosts
behaving like ghosts,
silent, affectless, odorless,
and then with real people
who slip into the room
to occupy the chairs
that shift under their human weight,
as if their absence was an error
that required correction.

We are the ones who tweak time,
who sit around, talk and clink glasses.
We putter about in our penultimate pages;
some thank their stars,
others pretend there are no stars
and carry on the graceful, oh so temporal,
organ recital until other sunny gripes
keep our eyes wide open.
Some of us are afraid to blink.

The Rabbit Explains

Aunt Tilly's grave site
is our playground;
do to our careful digging,
only love sifts through the soil.

The soft ground is not settled
though she's been in it
for generations.

There's a stone wall around the plots
and a paucity of peeking places
through which to see the chiseled marble.
Through one gap—half her name,
through another—a broken date.

We've been scraping the earth
forever, no malice, just our way
of being rabbits
to fling back the dirt
to expose the thought that had us hopping.
Then we bury it again
and our front paws relax.

We nose for wild flowers,
tender clover or crispy twigs—
delights among the markers.

Aunt Tilly's underground
longer now than she ever imagined.
We too travel that way
despite our fecund display.

It's in the Bag

The bag I live in has no holes,
except for the one large slit
there at the start.
As of now, the bag's struts
hold everything in place:
the calcified toes, the calluses,
the speckled run up to the knee,
the bone on bone; the bite that comes
suddenly or with a slow chew.

The skin, protector of the animal within
and its moving parts,
its plumbing, its throbbing heart
—excesses and setbacks—
is but a thin case,
a meager sack.

I've heard from those who measure and weigh
the bags—in my neighborhood at least—
they weigh less now than before,
and the progress towards weightlessness
while gradual, is a sure thing;
but at the same time,
the visible performance delights:
the dancer pretends to be outside the bag,
then it's pure form.

Listen to the Music

Performance Poems

Listen to the Music

When you come to my door
with that original smile,
wielding a bat with a smasharoo,
please do your damage
between noon and twilight,
time enough to change the day,
improve the outlook—for us both.

Please, at the end of my story—
a lament over slaughter,
explosions, slips of order,
background music to all past wars—
don't say, "small potatoes,"
and if you must mutter warnings,
let them come true but slowly.

Please be quiet down at the bar
with the music only measures away.
Piano, bass, drum and horn all hold
the echoes and the portents;
"The horror, the horror"—a drunk stutters—
and the jazzman says,
"compared to what?"

Lucky These Days

not to have been stung by bees
or gone broke on a bad bet
or tossed in a prison
with a cold narrow cot
for a minor something

lucky to be in front of you
or even seen by anyone near you
or no one—walking straight on a high hill
a thousand miles from home
lucky to be ambulatory
and lucky to have a home to return to

lucky to hear John's* piano
work its way along a register....
lucky to hear Vincent*
enriching this day...,
and Massimo's* bass lifts the hour....

lucky always to be in the music
lucky to have tasted the village
known the tastes of the village
lucky to have tasted you—
the smile of fortune at twilight

but luck has no future—only for
memories of generosity—

For now—it's notes ascending
colliding—So What (reference the tune)
the music's playing free
right here ....   [music plays out for 2-3 minutes]

*Vincent Chancey
*John Hicks
*Massimo Cavalli

Listening to Hal Galper at Club Bonafide
April, 2016

There's no melody he won't skirt.
When off the charted avenue
he finds—no, he plots and designs—
architecture with spires and arches
connecting nameless this to
wondrous that
outside the printed bars.

Listening to such originations,
the in-between tunes
on the ends of his fingers,
conceals the daily discordances,
filth and shame, and reveals instead
honey along the ivory keys.

Young players open the second set
with "I Cover the Waterfront."
He sketches the line, "I'm watching the sea,"
and then reaches for the "starry sky above."
None are deterred by the jazzman's substitutions
or where the melody might wander
beyond the club's protective boundary.

For John Hicks

December 21, 1941–May 10, 2006

Who are these people
who come to my table,
the food lean,
the beverage low in the glass?

They are seated now
annoying my time,
soiling the cloth, bending the utensils
chewing the ears off the plates.

One asks:
"what's that tune you're humming
by Benny Golson?"
"Domingo." It's the talk at the table
that makes me miss it from the stage.
"Domingo":
If anything swings,
it's Domingo
played by John Hicks.

Albert Ayler at the End of the Day

"...a melodist by nature" Valerie Wilmer

One says you shout,
another says you scream.
At the end of the day,
whoever speaks that way
misses the mark, trapped
in their own mechanics.

Albert Ayler blasted free
with the single-sided wonder, "Bells"
in '65 with Don Ayler, Charles Tyler,
Sunny Murray and Lewis Worrell—
drums and bass and brass
and the music charged:
martial struts and freedom ascending.

And at the end of the day
always the music—
still certainty, sweat & verve
and religious ease remixing technique
and love for the sounds and
who was with him.

At the end of the day
the man loved a round of golf.

At the end of the day
the muted scream silenced
drowned/ hush
pearls for eyes/ yes.

"Bomb Cyclone"

for Eric Plaks …

Music to step to /
this trio here /
they did the do for joyful time
the time we're in / they're in.

The lyrical slides
into percussive swing
led by ivory keys, double bass,
percussive everything.

Each measure finds the time
to cast aside the outside, the rumors
that brush the cheeks of babes
and oldsters too.

Conjure up heroes of Free Jazz /
the New Music
honed from the flesh of monsters:
The tradition that suckles this music.

A trio, a transport away
from all the terrors
that scrape along the chalkboard,
where this music glides instead.

Little Ditty

chinga locka changa
chinga locka cham
put me in the back seat
bam bam bam

chikka too chikka too
chikka too too too

the humming bird makes no sound
but for the whirring of wings—
the quick plunge of its beak into sweets
makes no sound

a rim a rack of wim wam
a rim a rack of soul
put me in the back seat
swirl swirl swirl

chikka too chikka too
chikka too too too

he's no humming bird
and he does make sounds, harsh at first
and protective, and then he whispers low—
when the comfort comes home

chikka boom chikka boom
kikka live live live
shift the car to drive
—now glide the back-seat home

Improvisation

Don't pity the one-legged man
for in the face of what binds us all
the loss of a limb,
like stomach distress,
is but a bruise on the rump of death.

don't pity the too tall man,
the 2-foot small `small person'
the woman who hides in the closet
the handsome man who sniffs her sheets
don't pity x or the y or the z
for in the face of our common bond,
the heat of our final fire,
the losses we name separately
are but hairs on the lip of Death

do pity the pickpocket
whose needs outweigh my own
but should I feel his hand again
I'd take it / I'd take it and shake it
and shake it off /
all he's ever known

now let's hear the music go sweet

no dark cloud
could break this spell in my heart
I'd spear that cloud
squeeze it into the bucket
toss it in the shed
lock it up
and
walk out under
the cold spell of winter sunshine.

Barry Wallenstein is the author of ten collections of poetry, the most recent being *Time on the Move* [Xanadu Press, 2020] and *Tony's Blues* (bilingual—French & English) [Éditions Pourquoi viens-tu si tard ? 2020], *Drastic Dislocations: New and Selected Poems* [NYQ Books, 2012]. His poetry has appeared in over 100 journals, including *Ploughshares, The Nation, American Poetry Review* and *New York Quarterly*.

The presentation of poetry readings in collaboration with jazz is a special interest. Barry Wallenstein has made eight recordings of his poetry with jazz, the most recent being titled *Lisbon Sunset,* (2016), *What Was, Was* [Audioscope, 2015] and *Lucky These Days* [Cadence Jazz Records 2013]. A previous CD, *Euphoria Ripens*, was listed among the "Best New Releases" in the journal, *All About Jazz* (December 2008).

Barry is Emeritus Professor of Literature and Creative Writing at the City University of New York and an editor of the journal, *American Book Review*.

www.barrywallenstein.com

www.ingramcontent.com/pod-product-compliance
Lightning Source LLC
Chambersburg PA
CBHW022011080426
42733CB00007B/561